DO YOU KNOW?

Level 4

WATER

Written by Adékúnmi Olátúnjí
Series Editor: Nick Coates
Designed by Dynamo Limited

LADYBIRD BOOKS

UK | USA | Canada | Ireland | Australia
India | New Zealand | South Africa

Ladybird Books Ltd is part of the Penguin Random House group of companies
whose addresses can be found at global.penguinrandomhouse.com.
www.penguin.co.uk   www.puffin.co.uk   www.ladybird.co.uk

Penguin
Random House
UK

First published 2023
001

Image on cover (iceberg) copyright © Niyazz/Shutterstock.com
image on page 1 (waterfall) copyright © Sharptoyou/Shutterstock.com
image on page 4 (deep) copyright © DOERS/Shutterstock.com
image on page 4 (desert) copyright © Alexxxey/Shutterstock.com
image on page 4 (float) copyright © Graphic design/Shutterstock.com
image on page 4 (flood) copyright © Wirestock Creators/Shutterstock.com
image on page 4 (glacier) copyright © VarnaK/Shutterstock.com
image on page 4 (lake) copyright © Boris Stroujko/Shutterstock.com
image on page 5 (melt) copyright © R Classen/Shutterstock.com
image on page 5 (microbe) copyright © Elif Bayraktar/Shutterstock.com
image on page 5 (pollution) copyright © Nady Ginzburg/Shutterstock.com
image on page 5 (scientist) copyright © PeopleImages.com - Yuri A/Shutterstock.com
image on page 5 (space) copyright © Aphelleon/Shutterstock.com
image on page 5 (temperature) copyright © Bjsites/Shutterstock.com
image on page 6 (spring) copyright © Designua/Shutterstock.com
image on page 6 and 7 (waterfall) copyright © Sharptoyou/Shutterstock.com
image on page 7 (water cycle) copyright © Alphabe/Shutterstock.com
image on page 8 (mussel) copyright © Goran Safarek/Shutterstock.com
image on page 8 (ragworm) copyright © Kukurund/Getty Images
image on page 8 and 9 (lakebed) copyright © Dudarev Mikhail/Shutterstock.com
image on page 9 (microbes) copyright © 3d_man/Shutterstock.com
image on page 9 (Lake Baikal) copyright © Strelyuk/Shutterstock.com
image on page 10 and 11 (Pink Lake) copyright © Matteo_it/Shutterstock.com
image on page 11 (Halobacteria) copyright © Power and Syred/Science Photo Library
image on page 11 (Dunaliella Salina) copyright © Steve Gschmeissner/Science Photo Library
image on page 11 (flamingo) copyright © Danita Delimont/Shutterstock.com
image on page 12 (macaques) copyright © Mapman/Shutterstock.com
image on page 12 and 13 (Grand Prismatic Spring, Yellowstone National Park) copyright © Lane V Erickson/Shutterstock.com
image on page 13 (Blood Pond Jigoku) copyright © Gritsalak Karalak/Shutterstock.com
image on page 14 and 15 (cave diver) copyright © Mauritius images GmbH/Alamy
image on page 15 (Horsetail Fall,) copyright © Gregory B Cuvelier/Shutterstock.com
image on page 16 (Anglerfish) copyright © Neil Bromhall/Shutterstock.com
image on page 16 and 17 (diver Mariana trench) copyright © DOERS/Shutterstock.com
image on page 17 (submarine) copyright © Ugo Sarto/AP/Shutterstock.com
image on page 17 (ocean pollution) copyright © Rich Carey/Shutterstock.com

image on page 18 (water on Mars) copyright © Pike-28/Shutterstock.com
image on page 18 (Moon) copyright © Fiona M. Donnelly/Shutterstock.com
image on page 18 and 19 (Solar System) copyright © Rwarnick/Getty Images
image on page 19 (ice on Moon) copyright © AP/Shutterstock.com
image on page 19 (water vapour) copyright © El Roce/Shutterstock.com
image on page 20 and 21 (man in Dead Sea) copyright © Crazy nook/Shutterstock.com
image on page 21 (Dead Sea) copyright © Vvvita/Shutterstock.com
image on page 21 (Dead Sea shrinking) copyright © FotoSajewicz/Shutterstock.com
image on page 22 and 23 (iceberg) copyright © Niyazz/Shutterstock.com
image on page 23 (world map) copyright © Volodymyr Nikulishyn/Shutterstock.com
image on page 23 (iceberg) copyright © Canadian Press/Shutterstock.com
image on page 23 (A-76 iceberg) copyright © ABACA/Shutterstock.com
image on page 23 (Hong Kong) copyright © Hamidah Samutharangkoon/Shutterstock.com
image on page 24 (elephants) copyright © Villiers Steyn/Shutterstock.com
image on page 24 and 25 (desert spring) copyright © Kertu/Shutterstock.com
image on page 25 (Crescent Lake) copyright © Liyuhan/Shutterstock.com
image on page 25 (Lake in Badain) copyright © Shutterstock.com
image on page 25 (Ruby Lake, Badain) copyright © Shutterstock.com
image on page 26 (Lake Chad from space) copyright © Space Frontiers/Archive Photos/Hulton Archive/Getty Images
image on page 26 and 27 (Lake Chad) copyright © Sia Kambou/AFP/Getty Images
image on page 27 (maps Lake Chad) copyright © Dynamo
image on page 27 (pollution from industry) copyright © Tr Stok/Shutterstock.com
image on page 28 and 29 (flood) copyright © Wirestock Creators/Shutterstock.com
image on page 29 (water cycle) copyright © Merkushev Vasiliy/Shutterstock.com
image on page 29 (coastal flood) copyright © Arthur Villator/Shutterstock.com
image on page 30 (spring) copyright © Designua/Shutterstock.com
image on page 30 (Lake Baikal) copyright © Strelyuk/Shutterstock.com
image on page 30 (Pink Lake) copyright © Shutterstock.com
image on page 30 (anglerfish) copyright © Neil Bromhall/Shutterstock.com
image on page 31 (Dead Sea) copyright © Vvvita/Shutterstock.com
image on page 31 (A-76 iceberg) copyright © ABACA/Shutterstock.com
image on page 31 (Lake Chad) copyright © Space Frontiers/Archive Photos/Hulton Archive/Getty Images
image on page 31 (flood) copyright © Wirestock Creators/Shutterstock

Printed in China

The authorized representative in the EEA is Penguin Random House Ireland,
Morrison Chambers, 32 Nassau Street, Dublin D02 YH68

A CIP catalogue record for this book is available from the British Library

ISBN: 978-0-241-62257-5

All correspondence to:
Ladybird Books
Penguin Random House Children's
One Embassy Gardens, 8 Viaduct Gardens, London SW11 7BW

FSC
www.fsc.org
MIX
Paper from
responsible sources
FSC® C018179

Contents

New words   4

Where do we find water?   6

What is at the bottom of a lake?   8

Can water be pink?   10

Why are hot springs hot?   12

What other colours can water be?   14

How deep is the Mariana Trench?   16

Is there water in space?   18

Why can people float in the Dead Sea?   20

How big is an iceberg?   22

Can deserts have water?   24

Where did Lake Chad go?   26

What happens in a flood?   28

Quiz   30

New words

deep

desert

float
(verb)

flood
(noun)

glacier

lake

melt

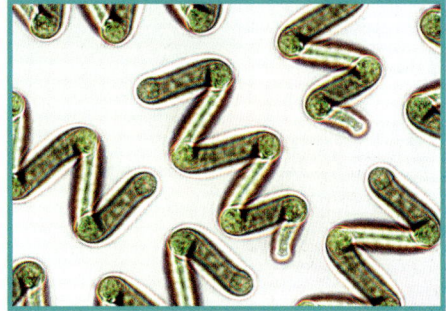

microbe

pollution

scientist

space

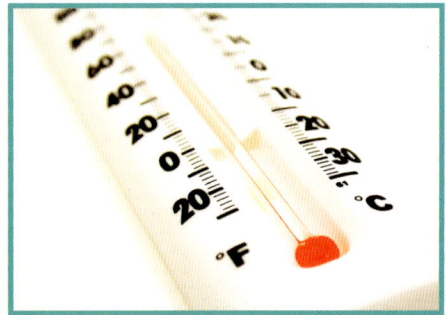

temperature

Where do we find water?

Most of the Earth is water. Water is in oceans, **lakes** and rivers. Water is in clouds, and it is in rain and snow. Ice is water, too! It is on the top of mountains and in **glaciers**.

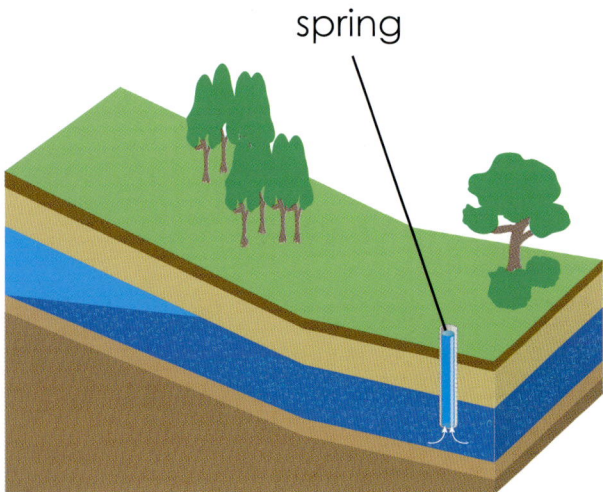

spring

There is also water under the ground. Water can come up and out of the ground as a spring.

water cycle

cloud

rain

vapour

lake

river

ocean

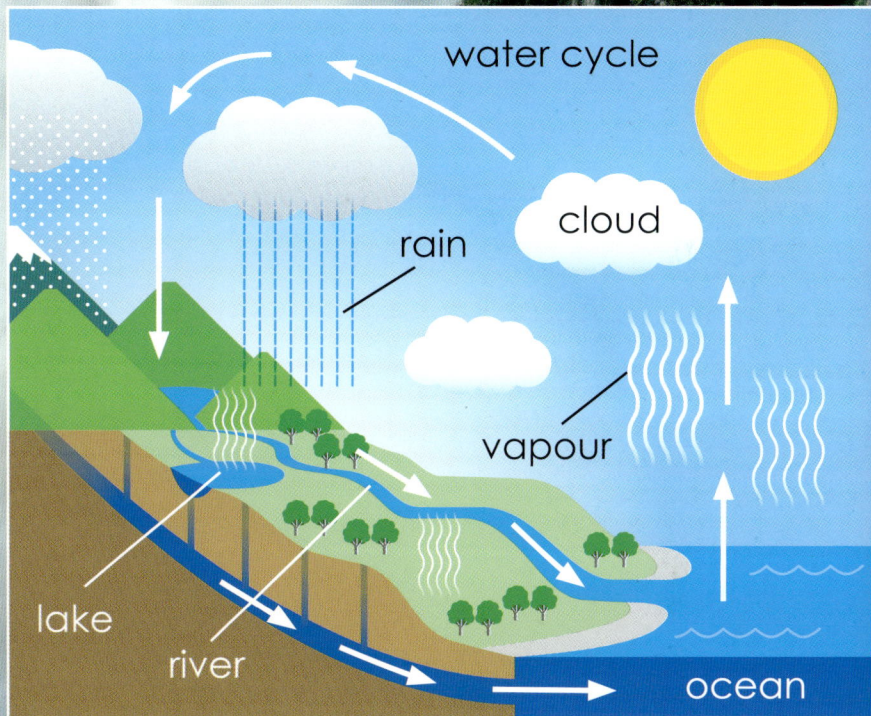

Water is always moving around the Earth in the water cycle. High **temperatures** change water into vapour. Cool temperatures change vapour into water.

📖 FIND OUT!

Use books or the internet. What is the name of the biggest ocean in the world?

What is at the bottom of a lake?

The bottom of a lake is the benthic zone. There is a lot of mud there. Plants grow and small animals live in the mud.

mussel

ragworm

benthic zone

microbes

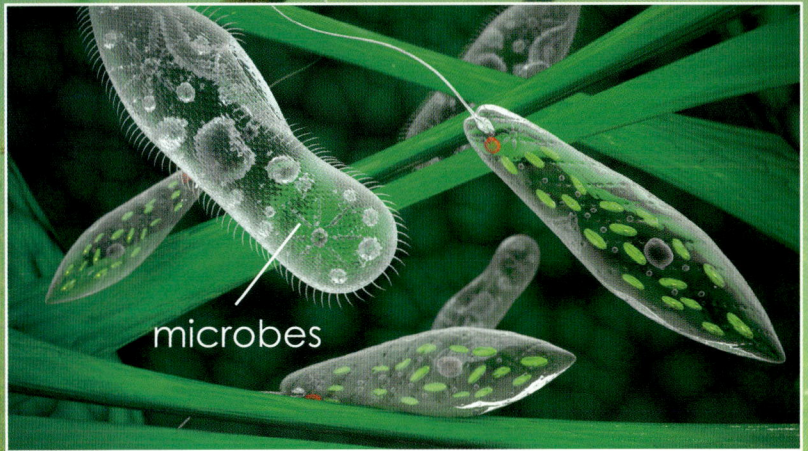

Microbes live in the benthic zone.
They eat dead plants and animals.

The oldest and deepest lake in the world is
Lake Baikal in Russia. The lake is more than
1,637 metres **deep** and about 25 million years old.
Scientists learn about the history of the Earth by
studying the bottom of this lake.

mud

💭 **THINK!**

Why do you think some lakes look
dark and others look clear?

Can water be pink?

Water often has no colour, but some lakes look pink. There are some microbes that live in water with a lot of salt, and pink lakes are full of salt. These microbes give the lake its pink colour.

Most pink lakes are not pink all the time. The colour changes in different months of the year because of the weather.

Pink Lake, Victoria, Australia

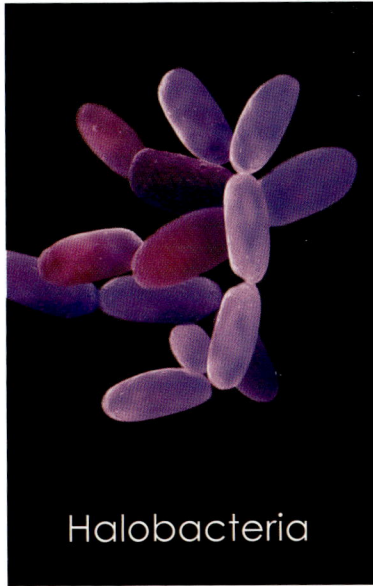

Halobacteria

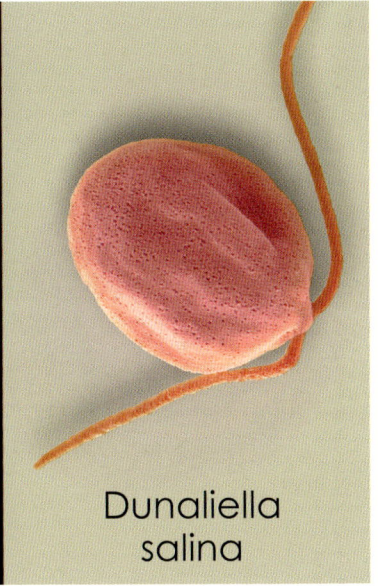

Dunaliella salina

Microbes colour the water pink.

— flamingo

The pink Lake Natron in Tanzania is home to pink flamingoes.

▶ WATCH!

Watch the video (see page 32).
What type of weather makes the lakes more colourful?
What can people do in the lake?

Why are hot springs hot?

There are very hot rocks inside the Earth. Water under the Earth moves around the rocks, and it gets hot, too. When this water comes up and out of the ground, we get a hot spring.

Some springs around the world have water that is good for you. People and some animals like to take a bath in hot springs.

Chinoike Jigoku (the 'blood pond') in Beppu, Japan is very hot. You can't take a bath in it. The water is so hot that it becomes vapour very quickly.

Grand Prismatic Spring, Yellowstone National Park, USA

📖 FIND OUT!

Use books or the internet. At what temperature does water easily become vapour?

What other colours can water be?

Water in the Santa Fe River is dark brown because trees in the river colour the water. The water in the Devil's Ear Spring has no colour but when the river and spring meet, the water becomes red. The light from the Sun adds yellow and orange colours.

under the water in Devil's Ear Spring, Florida, USA

Horsetail Fall, California, USA

The water in the Horsetail Fall can look red, orange and yellow in the Sun's light. This happens in February on an evening with no clouds.

🔍 LOOK!

Look at the pages. Sometimes the ocean can look red, orange and yellow. What time of day does this usually happen?

How deep is the Mariana Trench?

The deepest place on Earth is called the Mariana Trench. It is in the Pacific Ocean. It is about 11 kilometres deep! Big fish can't swim to the bottom of the trench. Only small animals live at the bottom.

anglerfish

People first went to the bottom of the trench in 1960.

Pollution in the oceans is a big problem. There are plastic bags at the bottom of the Mariana Trench now. Scientists have found sea animals with plastic in their stomachs.

▶ **WATCH!**

Watch the video (see page 32).
How long will it take to reach the bottom of the Mariana Trench?

Is there water in space?

Scientists have found water in **space**, but water in space is not the same as on Earth.

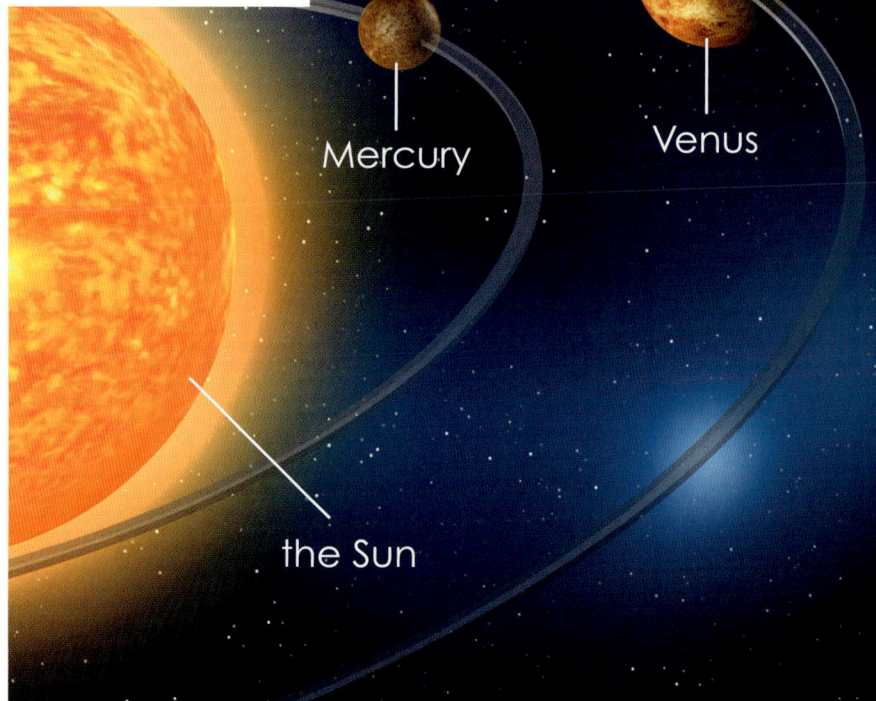

Earth

the Moon

Mercury

Venus

the Sun

There is water on Mars, but most of the water is ice. Some water on Mars is vapour.

Jupiter

Uranus

Neptune

Saturn

Mars

ocean

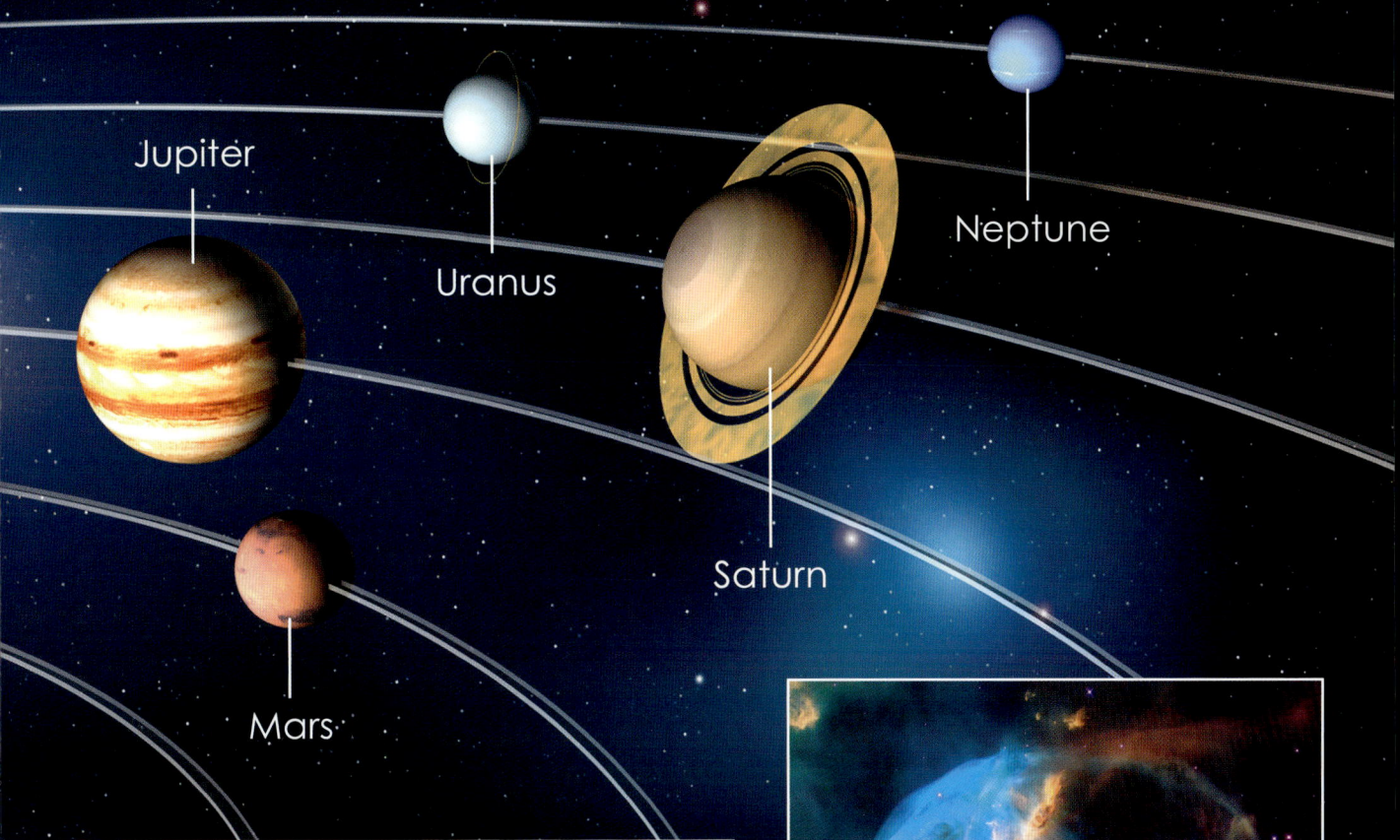

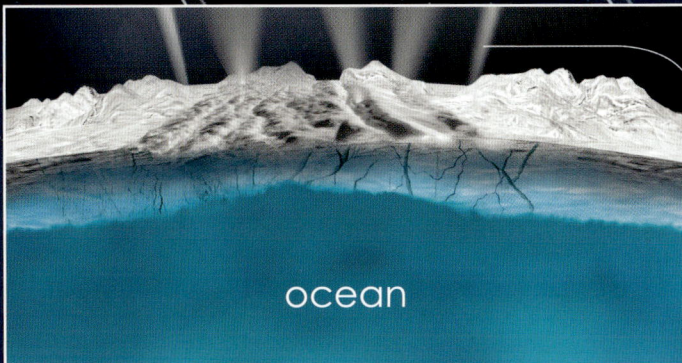

There is also ice on Earth's moon. Scientists think that other moons in space have large oceans on them. The oceans may be under ice.

Scientists have also found a very big cloud of water vapour in space. It is very far away from Earth.

💭 **THINK!**

Water is important for life on Earth. There is ice and water vapour in space. Do you think there is life in space?

Why can people float in the Dead Sea?

The Dead Sea is not really a sea – it is a lake. It is called 'Dead' because no fish or plants can live in it. This is because the lake is full of salt. The water is heavy because of the salt. Our bodies are not as heavy as the Dead Sea water, so we can **float** in it.

The Dead Sea

The Dead Sea is smaller than in the past. There is not enough water coming from the River Jordan and people take too much water. This makes the lake smaller.

PROJECT

Work with a friend to do this floating experiment. Pour water into a glass until it is about ¾ full. Add ½ cup of salt to the glass and stir. Put an egg into the glass and see what happens. What happens to the egg? Why do you think that is? Now, pour water into another glass until it is about ¾ full. Put an egg into the glass (with no salt). What happens to the egg now?

How big is an iceberg?

iceberg

When it is warm in spring, glaciers can **melt** and break. Pieces of the glaciers float away as icebergs.

It is difficult to see how big icebergs really are. Most of the ice is below the water.

Icebergs usually come from glaciers in Greenland and Antarctica. It is very cold there.

Greenland

Antarctica

Icebergs travel for many years before they melt.

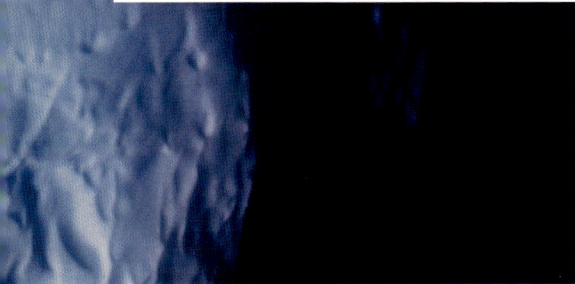

The world's biggest iceberg is called A-76. Scientists first saw it in May 2021. It is bigger than the city of Hong Kong!

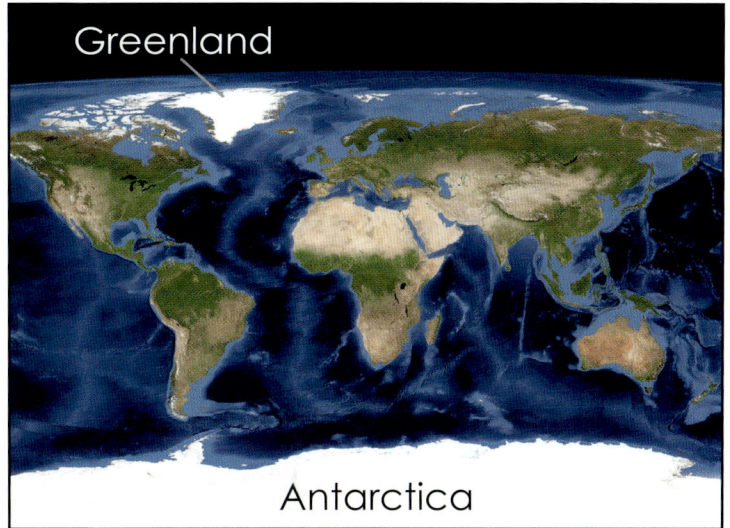

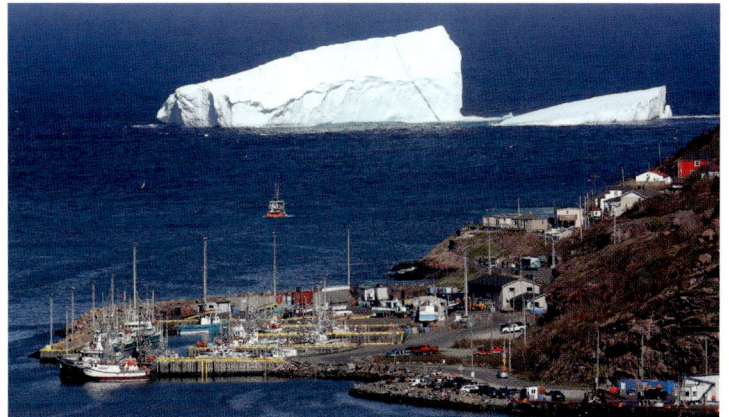

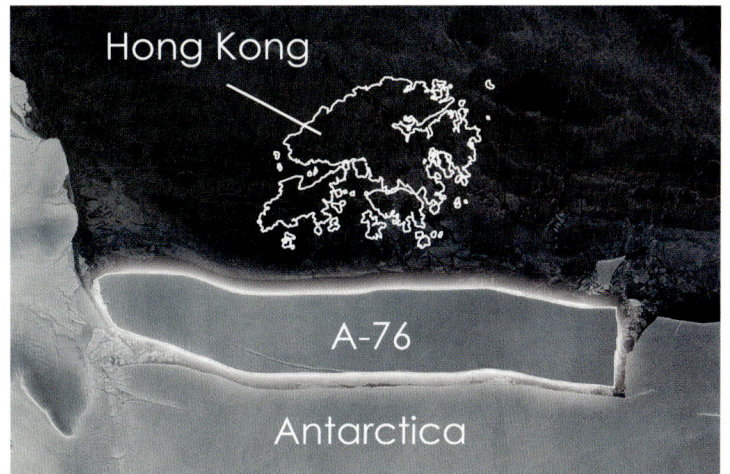

Hong Kong

A-76

Antarctica

📋 PROJECT

Work with a friend. Find out where the iceberg A-76 is now.

Can deserts have water?

Deserts are places that get very little rain. They can be very hot. They are empty and very dry. Sometimes it is possible to find water in the desert. This is a desert spring.

Near a desert spring, plants can grow and animals can eat and drink.

The Crescent Lake is a spring in a desert in China.

There are over 100 lakes in the Badain Jaran Desert in China. Some of the lakes change colour because of the salt, microbes and animals in them.

📖 FIND OUT!

Use books or the internet. What is the name of the area around a desert spring where plants grow?

Where did Lake Chad go?

Lake Chad is in West Africa. Many people use the lake to catch fish, grow food and get water for their animals to drink.

The weather has changed and only a little rain falls on Lake Chad now. The lake is smaller than in the past. This is a problem for millions of people.

Lake Chad

1963	2007
Chad	Chad
Niger	Niger
Nigeria	Nigeria
Cameroon	Cameroon

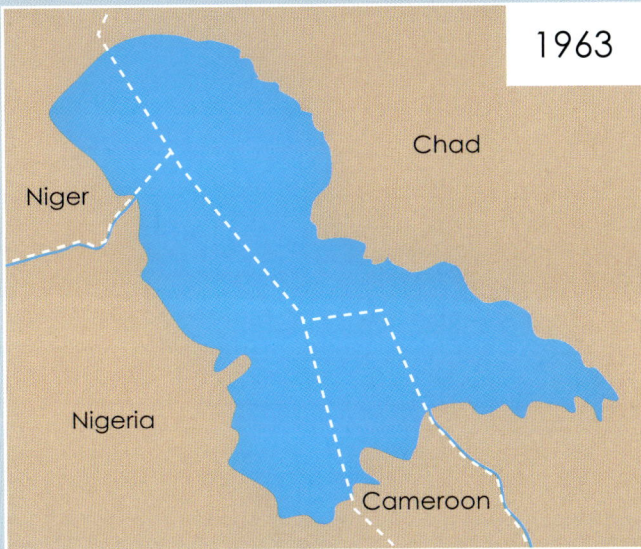

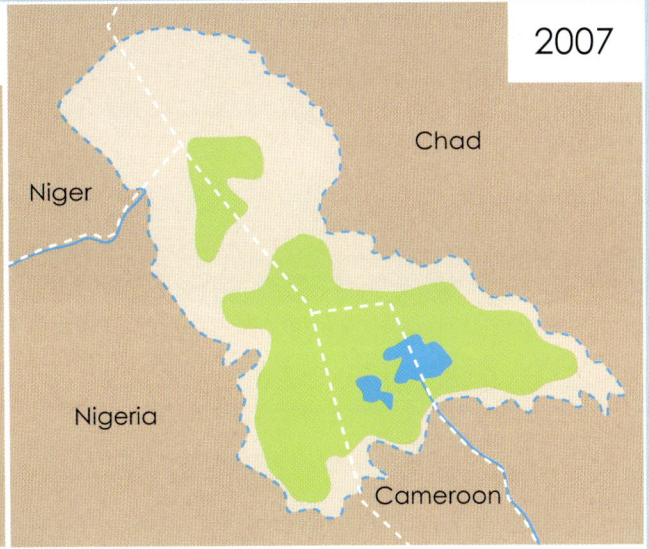

Lake Chad from 1963 to 2007.

Pollution makes the Earth warmer. Pollution from some countries changes the weather in other countries.

▶ WATCH!

Watch the video (see page 32).
Lake Chad is in which four countries? How big was Lake Chad 50 years ago in square kilometres? How big is it today?

What happens in a flood?

When rain falls, the water travels into lakes and rivers or goes into the ground. A **flood** happens when there is too much rain. Sometimes lakes and rivers become too full, or sometimes the ground becomes too wet.

Floods can be very dangerous. Sometimes people must leave their homes.

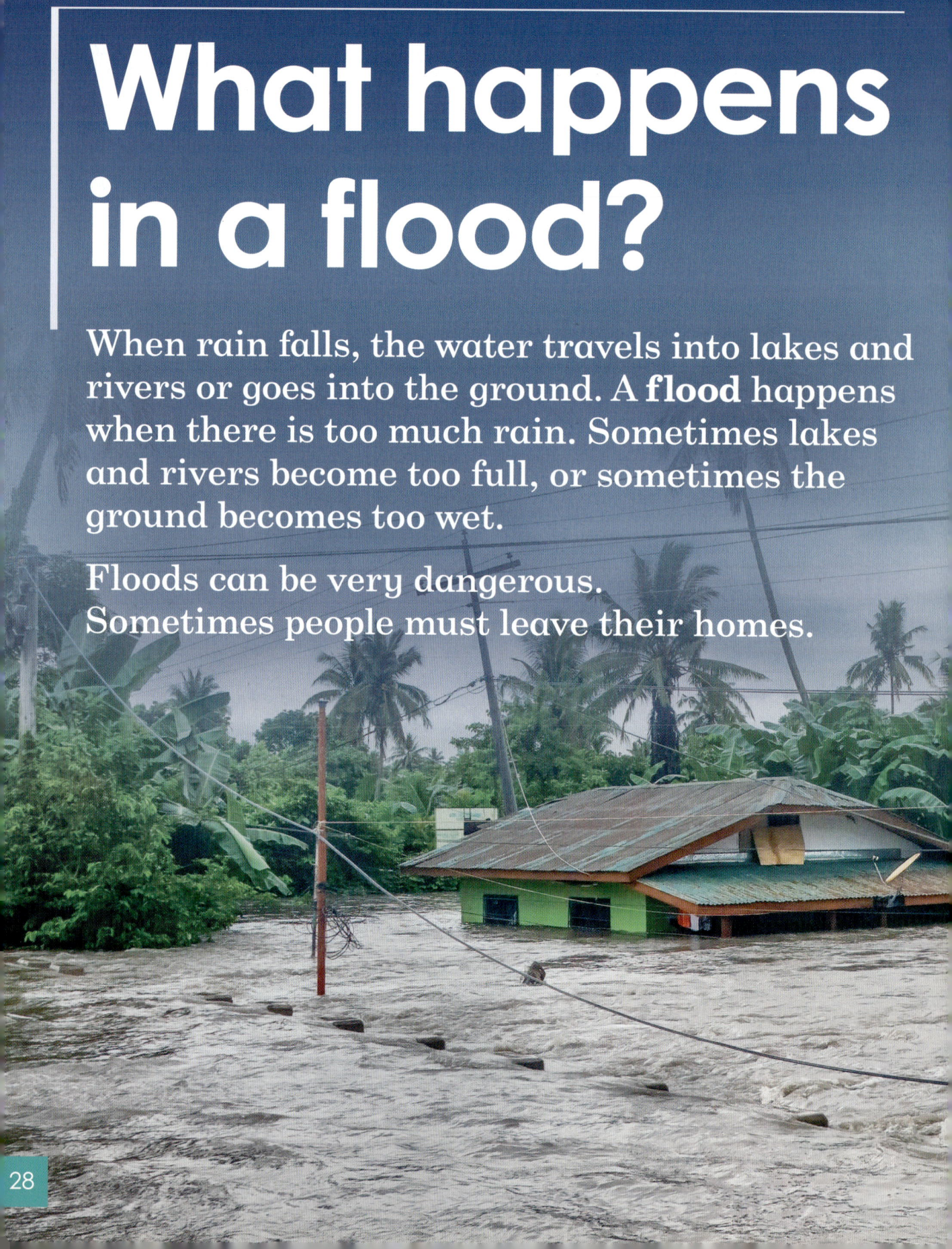

Floods happen more often now because the Earth has become warmer. The higher temperature changes the water cycle. Wet areas are now wetter.

Floods also happen in cities and towns by the sea. In the future, they may be under the water.

📋 PROJECT

Work with a friend. Find out what you should do if there is a flood where you live.

Quiz

Choose the correct answers.

1 Water can come up and out
of the ground as a . . .
  a lake.
  b plant.
  c spring.

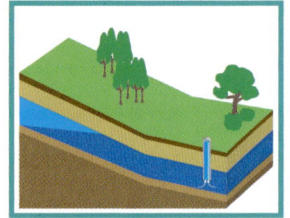

2 The oldest lake in the world is . . .
  a Lake Baikal.
  b Crescent Lake.
  c Lake Chad.

3 What makes a lake pink?
  a fish
  b microbes
  c plants

4 What lives at the bottom of the
Mariana Trench?
  a small animals
  b big fish
  c people

5 What does the Dead Sea
have a lot of?
  a plants
  b fish
  c salt

6 The world's biggest iceberg is called . . .
  a Hong Kong.
  b A-76.
  c Antarctica.

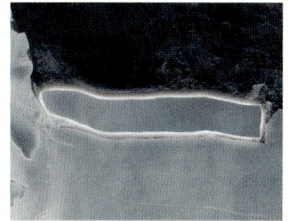

7 Where is Lake Chad?
  a West Africa
  b Greenland
  c Antarctica

8 Why do floods happen?
  a too much rain
  b too little rain
  c cold temperatures

DO YOU KNOW?

Visit www.ladybirdeducation.co.uk for
FREE **DO YOU KNOW?** teaching resources.

- video clips with simplified voiceover and subtitles
- video and comprehension activities
- class projects and lesson plans
- audio recording of every book
- digital version of every book
- full answer keys

To access video clips, audio tracks and digital books:

1 Go to **www.ladybirdeducation.co.uk**
2 Click 'Unlock book'
3 Enter the code below

itcDuKAeHH

Stay safe online! Some of the DO YOU KNOW? activities ask children to do extra research online. Remember:

- ensure an adult is supervising;
- use established search engines such as Google or Kiddle;
- children should never share personal details, such as name, home or school address, telephone number or photos.